❖ Golden India ❖

INDIAN RECIPES

❖ Golden India ❖
INDIAN RECIPES

Lustre Press
Roli Books

© Lustre Press Pvt. Ltd. 1996

First published by
Lustre Press Pvt. Ltd.
M-75, GK II Market,
New Delhi-110 048, INDIA
Phones: (011) 644 2271/646 2782/
646 0886/646 0887
Fax: (011) 646 7185

Acknowledgements

The publishers would like to thank Ms. Geeta Mathur for some of her recipes and her contribution in the making of this book.

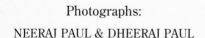

ISBN: 81-7437-049-8

Text Editor:
ARTI ARORA

Photographs:
NEERAJ PAUL & DHEERAJ PAUL

Processed at
Laser Graphics Pvt. Ltd.,
New Delhi

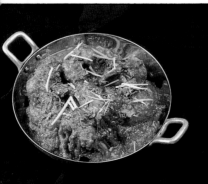

Printed and bound by
Star Standard Industries Pte. Ltd.,
Singapore

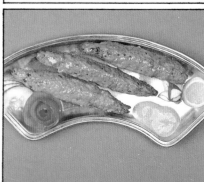

Conceived & Designed by
PRAMOD KAPOOR
at
ROLI BOOKS CAD CENTRE

Production:
N. K. NIGAM

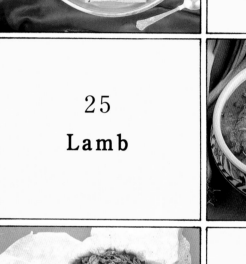

INTRODUCTION

The essence of **Indian Cuisine** lies in the variety of spices available and the aromas generated by their use. Diversity in climate, in cultures, social habits and the geographic locations contributes greatly to a vast variety of India's gastronomy. A lamb curry from Kashmir can be quite different from the one cooked in the neighbouring state of Punjab. Yet again, the same dish is cooked with coconut in the coastal state of Goa and in the desert state of Rajasthan, it becomes pungent with the use of chillies and strong spices. Food from each region therefore acquires its character from the availability of local spices and the eating habits of the region. **Indians clearly take great pride in their food.** Besides spices, another factor which contributes to the uniqueness of Indian food, is the wide range of **cooking methods** employed. The ever popular Tandoori Chicken, traditionally grilled on a charcoal fire, becomes even more exotic when it is cooked in a sealed casserole, on very low flame. This method is called *Dum Pukht* (cooking on low heat), which enables the food to mature in its own juices and the spices added to it. Deep frying in a *Kadhai* (Indian wok) and stir frying on a *Tawa* (griddle) are the other methods commonly used for the preparation of Indian dishes.

An assortment of Indian spices: (Clockwise from bottom) turmeric powder, coriander powder, cumin, green cardamoms and cloves, red chilli powder and whole dried coriander: (centre) salt.

Indian breads, usually accompanying the main dishes,

are well known the world over. *Naans* are baked in a *tandoor* or an oven, *Pooris* are deep fried in a *kadhai*, whereas, the *Rotis* and the *Paranthas* are roasted on a *tawa*. Quite often these breads are stuffed with mashed potatoes, boiled peas, grated *paneer* or even minced lamb to make them more exotic.

No Indian meal is complete without a sweet dish which traditionally, is served alongwith other dishes and not as the last course. Most Indian desserts are made out of milk, fruits or vegetables and tend to be sweeter as compared to the western ones. Desserts made out of milk are most common throughout India. The **presentation** of an Indian meal is as charming as its delicious taste. In an Indian meal, all the dishes are served at one time in a *Thali* (large circular plate) quite unlike the system of several courses as followed in most countries. In a *thali* the curries are served in several *Katoris* (small bowls) and the dry dishes and breads are served direct on it. The presentation of food also differs from one region to another. The use of Banana leaf to serve the food on, is not very uncommon in the coastal areas. In the plains, plates made of dry leaves are still used in the villages.

Indian food has increasingly become **popular** throughout the world. The restaurants all over the world have fine-tuned the regional recipes to suit the local tastes. Easy availability of the various ingredients used in Indian kitchens, in majority of the stores, only adds to the charm.

So go ahead and treat yourself ! ! !

A traditional Indian Thali meal, complete with dry and curry dishes, accompaniments and dessert.

CHICKEN KEBAB

Barbecued chicken cubes.

Serves: 4-5   **Preparation time:** 5 hours   **Cooking time:** 10 minutes

INGREDIENTS:

Chicken (cut into boneless cubes) .... *1 kg*
Black pepper, crushed .... *5 gms / 1 tsp*
Butter or oil for basting
Coriander, ground .... *15 gms / 1 tbs*
Cumin powder .... *5 gms / 1 tsp*
Double cream .... *60 ml / 4 tbs*

Garlic paste .... *40 gms / $2^2/_3$ tbs*
Ginger, finely chopped .... *50 gms / $3^1/_3$ tbs*
Green chilli paste .... *10 gms / 2 tsp*
Onion (small), finely grated *2*
Salt to taste
Yoghurt .... *200 gms / 1 cup*

METHOD:

1. Combine the yoghurt, cream, grated onion, garlic, ginger and chilli pastes, ground coriander, cumin, black pepper powder and salt together.
2. Add the chicken cubes to the marinade and mix well. Cover the bowl and chill in the refrigerator for at least 3-4 hrs.
3. Preheat the grill to 175 °C (350 °F).
4. Skewer the chicken cubes 2 cms apart and place skewers in a grill or roast in a tandoor for 5-8 minutes.
5. Baste with butter/oil and roast for another 3 minutes or until they are cooked through.
6. Remove from skewers and garnish with onion rings, tomato slices and chopped coriander.

TO SERVE:

Serve hot, on a bed of rice accompanied by
Mint chutney (page 83).

TANGRI KEBAB

Barbecued chicken drumsticks.

Serves: 4-5   **Preparation time:** 3-4 hours   **Cooking time:** 15-20 minutes

INGREDIENTS:

Chicken drumsticks (skinless) 15	Ginger paste .... *20 gms / 4 tsp*
Butter/oil for basting	Lemon juice .... *25 ml / 5 tsp*
Cumin powder, roasted .... *5 gms / 1 tsp*	Red chilli powder .... *7 gms / 1½ tsp*
Garam masala .... *10 gms / 2 tsp*	Salt to taste
Garlic paste .... *20 gms / 4 tsp*	Yoghurt .... *200 gms / 1 cup*

METHOD:

1. Make 2 incisions on each drumstick.
2. Rub lemon juice into the drumsticks. Set aside for 20 minutes.
3. Mix all ingredients except butter/oil into the yoghurt and mix well.
4. Add chicken to the marinade and coat the pieces evenly.
   Set aside for 2-3 hrs.
5. Preheat oven/grill to 175 °C (350 °F).
6. Skewer drumsticks 2 cm apart and roast/grill in tandoor/oven for 10-12 minutes. Baste with melted butter/oil 2-3 times. Roast until golden brown in colour.

TO SERVE:

Serve hot on a bed of shredded lettuce/cabbage garnished with onion rings, tomato slices and lemon wedges.

Mustard Chicken Tikka

Chicken kebab, uniquely flavoured with mustard.

Serves: 4   **Prep. time:** 4 hrs   **Cooking time:** 10 min

Ingredients:

Chicken (cut into boneless cubes) .... *1 kg*
Garlic paste .... *45 gms / 3 tbs*
Ginger paste .... *45 gms/ 3 tbs*
Gram flour .... *20 gms / 4 tsp*
Green chillies, deseeded and chopped *4*
Lemon juice .... *60 ml / 4 tbs*
Mustard oil (*sarson ka tel*) .... *45 ml / 3 tbs*
Mustard paste (medium sharp) ....*30 gms / 2 tbs*
Salt to taste
Yellow chilli powder .... *5 gms / 1 tsp*
Yoghurt, drained .... *50 gms / 3¹/₃ tbs*

Method:

1. Mix together ginger, garlic and mustard pastes, salt and lemon juice.
2. Rub over the chicken evenly. Keep aside for 15 minutes.
3. Whisk yoghurt in a large bowl. Add the remaining ingredients and mix well. Coat the chicken pieces with this mixture. Keep aside for 3½ hours.
4. Preheat oven to 175 °C (350 °F).
5. Skewer the marinated chicken and roast in oven for 8-10 minutes, basting with mustard oil (preferably) at least twice.

To Serve:

Serve hot, garnished with lemon wedges, accompanied by green salad and Mint chutney (page 83).

Spiced Fried Chicken

Pan-cooked chicken kebab.

Serves: 6   **Prep time:** 45 min   **Cooking time:** 30-45 min

Ingredients:

Chicken (boneless, cubed and boiled) .... *1 kg*
Garam masala .... *5 gms / 1 tsp*
Garlic paste .... *15 gms / 1 tbs*
Ginger paste .... *15 gms / 1 tbs*
Oil .... *45 ml / 3 tbs*
Onion, sliced *1*
Red chilli powder .... *2½ gms / ½ tsp*
Red colour .... *2 gms / ¼ tsp*
Salt to taste
Turmeric powder .... *3 gms / ½ tsp*
Yoghurt .... *100 gms/ ½ cup*

Method:

1. Mix chicken with yoghurt, ginger and garlic pastes and all other ingredients except oil and sliced onions. Keep aside for 30 minutes.
2. Heat oil in a pan, sauté onion slices till transparent, add chicken and fry on low flame till all liquids are absorbed and kebabs are fragrant and crisp.

To Serve:

Sprinkle lemon juice and serve hot, garnished with chopped coriander and onion slices.

GARLIC CHICKEN KEBABS

Marinated chicken kebabs with the pungent flavour of garlic.

Serves: 4-5   **Preparation time:** 3-4 hours   **Cooking time:** 12-15 minutes

INGREDIENTS:

Chicken (cut into boneless cubes) .... *1 kg*
Black pepper, crushed .... *5 gms / 1 tsp*
Cheese, grated .... *60 gms / 4 tbs*
Coriander powder .... *5 gms / 1 tsp*
Cumin seeds, roasted and powdered .... *5 gms / 1 tsp*
Double cream............................... *60 ml / 4 tbs*
Garlic, coarsely pounded .... *100 gms / ½ cup*

Garlic paste .... *40 gms / 2²/₃ tbs*
Ginger paste .... *45 gms / 3 tbs*
Green chilli paste....................................... *15 gms / 1 tbs*
Lemon juice .... *15 ml / 1 tbs*
Salt to taste
Yoghurt.. *200 gms / 1 cup*

METHOD:

1. Rub lemon juice into the chicken and set aside for 20 minutes, then pat dry.
2. Mix yoghurt, cheese, double cream, cumin powder, black pepper, coriander powder, salt, garlic paste, ginger and green chilli pastes.
3. Coat the chicken pieces with the above marinade and leave in the refrigerator for 3-4 hours.
4. Preheat oven/grill to 175 °C (350 °F).
5. Skewer chicken pieces 2 cm apart. Press the pounded garlic onto the chicken and roast/grill for 5-8 minutes.
6. Baste with butter/oil and roast for another 3-4 minutes or until cooked through and golden brown in colour.

TO SERVE:

Serve hot, garnished with onion rings, sliced cucumber and chopped coriander, accompanied by Mint chutney (page 83).

13

TANDOORI CHICKEN

The most popular of Indian Cuisine, a succulent, mildly spiced, grilled chicken dish.

Serves: 4   **Preparation time:** 6 hours   **Cooking time:** 25 minutes

INGREDIENTS:

Chicken broiler (skinless)
(600 gms each) 2
Butter, for basting .... *50 gms / ¼ cup*
Chaat masala .... *5 gms / 1 tsp*
Cream .... *10 ml / 2 tsp*
Garlic paste .... *50 gms / 3¹/₃ tbs*
Ginger paste .... *10 gms / 2 tsp*
Lemon juice .... *30 ml / 2 tbs*
Red chilli paste .... *25 gms / 5 tsp*
Salt to taste

For the marinade:
Cumin powder (*jeera*) .... *5 gms / 1 tsp*
Garam masala .... *10 gms / 2 tsp*
Ginger paste .... *25 gms / 5 tsp*
Lemon juice .... *30 ml / 2 tbs*
Oil .... *50 ml / 3¹/₃ tbs*
Red chilli paste .... *25 gms / 5 tsp*
Saffron .... *few strands*
Salt to taste
Yoghurt, drained .... *200 gms / 1 cup*

METHOD:

1. Make incisions—3 each on breasts and thighs and 2 each on drumsticks.
2. Mix the salt, red chilli paste, ginger and garlic pastes and lemon juice, rub this paste into the chicken. Keep aside for 30 minutes.
3. Whisk yoghurt in a large bowl and mix all the ingredients for the marinade.
4. Coat the chicken with the marinade and leave in the refrigerator for 5-6 hours.
5. Preheat the oven or tandoor to 175 ℃ (350 ℉).
6. Skewer the chickens from head to tail, leaving a 4 cm gap between each. Keep a tray underneath to collect excess drippings.
7. Roast approximately for 15 minutes or until almost done. Remove and baste with butter, then roast for another 5 minutes.

TO SERVE:

Remove the chicken from the skewer, cut each into four pieces and arrange on a platter. Sprinkle chaat masala and cream, garnish with raw onion rings and lemon wedges and serve hot.

Reshmi Kebab

An extra smooth chicken mince kebab.

Serves: 4   **Preparation time:** 30 minutes   **Cooking time:** 6 minutes

Ingredients:

Chicken mince .... *1 kg*	Ginger, finely chopped .... *30 gms / 2 tbs*
Butter (unsalted) for brushing	Oil .... *20 ml / 4 tsp*
Cashewnuts, pounded .... *60 gms / 4 tbs*	Oil for basting
Coriander leaves, finely chopped .... *20 gms / 4 tsp*	Onions, finely chopped .... *20 gms / 4 tsp*
Cumin (*jeera*) powder .... *15 gms / 1 tbs*	Salt to taste
Eggs *2*	White pepper powder .... *5 gms / 1 tsp*
Garam masala .... *5 gms / 1 tsp*	Yellow chilli powder .... *5 gms / 1 tsp*

Method:

1. Whisk the eggs, add cumin powder, yellow chilli powder, white pepper powder, salt and oil. Add to the mince and mix well. Set aside for 10 minutes.
2. Add cashewnuts, ginger, onions, coriander and garam masala. Mix well.
3. Divide into 10 equal portions.
4. Wrap two portions along each skewer using wet hands.
   Keep 2 inches between each portion. Prepare 5 skewers like this.
5. Roast in a moderately hot tandoor or charcoal grill until golden brown in colour, about 6 minutes or roast in a preheated oven at 150 °C (300 °F) for 8 minutes, basting with oil just once.
6. Remove from skewers and brush with butter.

To Serve:

Serve hot, garnished with onion rings and lemon wedges.

KADHAI CHICKEN

Chicken cooked in a spicy tomato gravy.

Serves: 4   **Preparation time:** 30 minutes   **Cooking time:** 30 minutes

INGREDIENTS:

Chicken (cut into 12 pieces) .... *1 kg*
Garam masala .... *5 gms / 1 tsp*
Garlic paste .... *20 gms / 4 tsp*
Ginger, chopped .... *50 gms / 3²/₃ tbs*
Green chillies, sliced *2*

Oil .... *100 ml / ½ cup*
Red and Green Bell peppers .... *115 gms / 1 cup*
Red chilli, pounded coarsely *6-8*
Tomatoes, blanched and chopped .... *1 kg*

METHOD:

1. Heat oil in a *kadhai* (wok), sauté garlic paste, add red chillies, fry a while, add chopped tomatoes and cook for 5 minutes, stirring constantly.
2. Add ginger, sliced green chillies and salt, cook on medium heat for 3-5 minutes.

3. Add chicken pieces and cook till the gravy is thick and the chicken is tender.
4. Stir in red and green peppers, garam masala. Cover and cook for 3-4 minutes.

TO SERVE:

Garnish with chopped coriander and serve hot,
accompanied by Naan (page 75) or Chappati (page 75).

BUTTER CHICKEN

Roasted chicken in a rich creamy gravy.

Serves: 4   **Prep. time:** 20 min   **Cooking time:** 50 min

INGREDIENTS:

*Pre-cooked Tandoori chicken
cut into 8 pieces each .... *1 kg / 2 birds*
Butter .... *100 gms / ½ cup*
Coriander leaves, chopped .... *15 gms / 1 tbs*
Cream .... *160 ml / ²/₃ cup*
Garlic paste .... *45 gms /3 tbs*
Ginger paste .... *45 gms / 3 tbs*
Ginger, shredded .... *10 gms / 2 tsp*
Green chillies *5*
Paprika .... *2½ gms / ½ tsp*
Salt to taste
Tomatoes, chopped and blended .... *900 gms*
Water .... *480 ml / 2 cups*

METHOD:

* For Tandoori Chicken turn to page 15
1. Melt half the butter in a pan, add the ginger and garlic pastes, cook till the mixture is dry.
2. Add the blended tomatoes and salt, Add water, bring to a boil, simmer for a few minutes. Keep aside.
3. Melt the remaining butter in a *kadhai* (wok), add shredded ginger, green chillies and sauté for a minute. Add paprika, wait for the mixture to turn bright red.
4. Stir in the gravy, bring to a boil. Add the chicken pieces, simmer for 10 min. or until the chicken is tender.

TO SERVE:

Stir in the cream and serve hot, garnished with chopped coriander and accompanied by any Indian bread.

STIR FRIED CHICKEN

Shredded chicken with chillies.

Serves: 4-5   **Prep. time:** 5 hrs   **Cooking time:** 20 mins

INGREDIENTS:

Chicken (shredded) .... *1 kg*
Black pepper powder .... *5 gms / 1 tsp*
Garlic paste .... *50 gms / 3¹/₃ tbs*
Ginger paste .... *50 gms / 3¹/₃ tbs*
Lemon juice .... *30 ml / 2 tbs*
Oil .... *100 ml / ½ cup*
Red and green chillies (slit in half) *10*
Salt to taste
Spring onions, chopped in rounds .... *200 gms / 1 cup*
Water/chicken stock .... *100 ml / ½ cup*

METHOD:

1. Mix together ginger and garlic pastes, red chilli powder, salt and oil.
2. Add the shredded chicken to the marinade and chill in refrigerator for 4-5 hrs.
3. Heat oil in a *kadhai* (wok) and stir fry the chicken on high heat for 7-10 min.
4. Add chicken stock/water and continue stirring.
5. Add red and green chillies and spring onions. Stir and cook for another 3-5 minutes on medium heat.

TO SERVE:

Stir in the black pepper and lemon juice.
Serve hot, garnished with chopped coriander.

CHICKEN WITH SPINACH

Chicken curried in a spicy spinach purée.

Serves: 4-5 **Preparation time:** 10 minutes **Cooking time:** 45 minutes

INGREDIENTS:

Chicken, (skinned, cleaned and cut into pieces) .... *1 kg*
Bay leaves (*tej patta*) *2*
Butter .... *100 gms / ½ cup*
Cinnamon sticks *4*
Fenugreek powder (*methi*) .... *3 gms / ²/₃ tsp*
Garlic paste .... *40 gms / 2²/₃ tbs*
Ginger, julienned .... *10 gms / 2 tsp*
Ginger paste .... *40 gms / 2²/₃ tbs*
Maize flour (*makke ka atta*) .... *3 gms / ²/₃ tsp*

Oil .... *60 ml / 4 tbs*
Onion paste .... *200 gms / 1 cup*
Red chilli powder .... *10 gms / 2 tsp*
Salt to taste
Spinach (*palak*), puréed .... *350 gms / 1¾ cups*
Tomatoes, chopped .... *180 gms / ¾ cup*
Water .... *40 ml / 2²/₃ tbs*
White pepper powder .... *3 gms / ²/₃ tsp*

METHOD:

1. Heat oil in a pan, add whole spices (cinnamon and bay leaves), and sauté over medium heat until they begin to crackle.
2. Add the ginger, garlic and onion pastes and red chilli powder, stir fry for 30-60 seconds.
3. Add tomatoes and sauté further for 1 minute.
4. Add the spinach purée, stir in maize flour diluted with water and cook over medium heat for 10-15 minutes, stirring occasionally.
5. In another pan heat the butter and sauté the chicken until lightly browned.
6. Transfer the chicken pieces into the spinach sauce. Add salt and white pepper powder, cover and simmer on very low flame (*dum*) for 10-15 minutes or until chicken is cooked.

TO SERVE:

Serve hot, garnished with julienned ginger and fenugreek powder.

CHICKEN BADAM PASANDA

Chicken steaks in an almond flavoured sauce.

Serves: 4-5   **Preparation time:** 2½ hours   **Cooking time:** 30 minutes

INGREDIENTS:

Chicken breasts (medium size), cleaned, flattened .... *10 pcs*
Almonds, blanched and sliced .... *50 gms / ½ cup*
Chicken stock .... *340 ml / 1¾ cups*
Cloves *8-10*
Coriander, chopped (optional) .... *20 gms / 4 tsp*
Corn flour .... *15 gms / 1 tbs*
Garlic paste .... *45 gms / 3 tbs*
Ginger paste .... *45 gms / 3 tbs*

Green cardamoms *5-6*
Oil .... *210 ml / 1¼ cup*
Onions (medium sized), finely chopped *2*
Saffron, dissolved in 1 tsp milk .... *1 gm*
Salt to taste
White pepper powder .... *5 gms / 1 tsp*
Yoghurt .... *200 gms / 1 cup*

METHOD:

1. Keep aside 6-7 blanched almonds. Grind the rest into a paste and keep aside.
2. Rub ginger and garlic pastes into the steaks. Whisk yoghurt and salt together in a bowl and coat the chicken pieces evenly with it. Keep aside for 2 hours.
3. Heat oil in a pan and fry the steaks till almost done. Remove and keep aside.
4. In the same oil, sauté onions, cardamoms and cloves. Stir in the almond paste, fry a while, then add white pepper powder, chicken stock and flour. Cook till the gravy is rich, smooth and thick.
5. Remove from fire, strain the sauce to remove whole spices and reheat.
6. Add the steaks to the gravy and let it simmer for 10 mins or until the chicken is tender. Add dissolved saffron.

TO SERVE:

Garnish with sliced almonds and chopped coriander
(optional). Serve hot, accompanied by Naan (page 75)
or Parantha (page 76).

Seekh Kebab

Skewered minced lamb kebabs.

Serves: 4-5   **Preparation time:** 25 minutes   **Cooking time:** 15 minutes

Ingredients:

Lamb, minced .... *900 gms / 4½ cups*	Green chillies, finely chopped .... *8 gms / 1²/₃ tsp*
Green coriander, finely chopped .... *10 gms / 2 tsp*	Lamb kidney fat .... *150 gms / ¾ cup*
Butter to baste .... *50 gms / 3¹/₃ tbs*	Mace powder (*javitri*) .... *5 gms / 1 tsp*
Cardamom powder .... *3 gms / ²/₃ tsp*	Onion paste, browned .... *100 gms / ½ cup*
Cottage cheese (*paneer*), grated .... *15 gms / 3 tsp*	Poppy seed (*khus khus*) paste .... *100 gms / ½ cup*
Garam masala .... *20 gms / 4 tsp*	Salt to taste
Ginger paste .... *40 gms / 2²/₃ tbs*	

Method:

* For recipe of paneer see page 57

1. Combine all the ingredients in a bowl, mix thoroughly and refrigerate for 15 minutes.
2. Divide into 20 equal portions and roll into balls.
3. Preheat oven to 175 ˚C (350 ˚F).
4. Skewer each ball. Spread by pressing each, along the length of the skewer with a wet hand, making each kebab 8-10 cms long, 4 cms apart.
5. Roast in a hot tandoor or oven or charcoal grill for 8-10 minutes.
6. Remove and hang the skewers to let the excess moisture drip off.
7. Baste with butter and roast for another 2 minutes.

> ### To Serve:
> Garnish with sliced cucumber, tomato slices and onion rings. Serve hot, accompanied by Mint chutney (page 83).

SHOLA KEBAB

Succulent pieces of lamb barbecued to perfection.

Serves: 4-5   **Preparation time:** 6-7 hours   **Cooking time:** 10 minutes

INGREDIENTS:

Lamb (leg piece, chopped in boneless pieces) .... *1 kg*
Chilli powder .... *3 gms / ½ tsp*
Coriander powder .... *10 gms / 2 tsp*
Garlic paste .... *25 gms / 5 tsp*
Ginger paste .... *25 gms / 5 tsp*

Oil for basting
Salt to taste
Turmeric powder .... *10 gms / 2 tsp*
Yoghurt .... *150 ml / ²/₃ cup*

METHOD:

1. Mix together yoghurt, coriander powder, turmeric, chilli powder, ginger and garlic pastes and salt.
2. Pour mixture over lamb and coat the pieces evenly.
3. Baste the marinated pieces with oil and cover the bowl. Chill in refrigerator for 5-6 hrs, basting occasionally.
4. Preheat grill/oven to 175 °C (350 °C).
5. Mix meat marinade well, then skewer the pieces 2 cm apart.
6. Roast in tandoor/grill for 5-8 minutes on each side or until cooked through, basting just once.

TO SERVE:

Serve hot on a warmed serving dish garnished with onion rings, chopped coriander and lemon wedges, accompanied by Mint chutney (see page 83).

Peshawari Kebab

Succulent lamb pieces coated with raw papaya and yoghurt.

Serves: 4   **Preparation time:** 1¼ hours   **Cooking time:** 30 minutes

Ingredients:

Lamb (cut into boneless cubes) .... *1 kg*
Black cumin (*shah jeera*) seeds .... *5 gms / 1 tsp*
Chaat masala .... *5 gms / 1 tsp*
Clarified butter (*ghee*) for basting
Garam masala .... *5 gms / 1 tsp*
Garlic paste .... *5 gms / 1 tsp*

Ginger paste .... *15 gms / 1 tbs*
Lemon juice .... *7 gms / 1½ tsp*
Raw papaya paste .... *10 gms / 2 tsp*
Red chilli powder .... *10 gms / 2 tsp*
Salt to taste
Yoghurt .... *120 gms / ½ cup*

Method:

1. Mix together, salt, red chilli powder, garam masala, papaya paste, black cumin, ginger and garlic pastes and yoghurt.
2. Marinade lamb cubes in mixture and put aside for 1 hour.

3. Skewer lamb cubes 2 cms apart and cook in a tandoor till half done. Leave to cool for 10 minutes.
4. Baste with clarified butter (*ghee*) and roast for 8 more minutes or until done.

To Serve:

Sprinkle chaat masala and lemon juice.
Serve hot, accompanied by a green salad.

COCKTAIL KEBABS

Minced lamb kebabs, an ideal snack.

Serves: 4-6   **Preparation time:** 1½ hours   **Cooking time:** 30 minutes

INGREDIENTS:

Lamb, minced .... *½ kg*
Egg, slightly beaten *1*
Garam masala .... *8 gms / 1½ tsp*
Ginger, chopped .... *10 gms / 2 tsp*
Oil for frying
Onions (medium), chopped *2*
Red chillies, dried and chopped *4-5*
Salt to taste

Split grams (*chana daal*) .... *115 gms / ½ cup*

For the Stuffing:
Coriander leaves, chopped .... *6 gms / 1¹/₃ tsp*
Green chillies, finely chopped .... *15 gms / 1 tbs*
Onions, finely chopped .... *60 gms / 4 tbs*
Salt to taste

METHOD:

1. Boil minced meat along with split grams, red chillies, onions, salt and ginger in 4 cups of water till meat and gram is tender. Strain the liquid completely.
2. Grind the mince very finely, add the garam masala powder and beaten egg and knead well. Divide into 20 equal portions and keep aside.
3. In a separate bowl, mix chopped onions, green chillies, coriander leaves, salt and divide into 20 equal parts.
4. Flatten each part of the mince, put one part of stuffing into the centre and shape into a ball, wetting hands with water.
5. Heat oil in flat pan till it is smoking hot. Deep fry kebabs, a few at a time till crispy and brown.

TO SERVE:

Serve hot, garnished with onion rings and accompanied by Mint chutney (page 83).

Gosht Chaap Achari

Lamb chops cooked with whole spices.

Serves: 4-5   **Prep time:** 2½ hours   **Cooking time:** 30 minutes

Ingredients:

Lamb chops .... *8 pieces*	Lemon juice .... *15 ml / 1 tbs*
Aniseed .... *5 gms / 1 tsp*	Meat tenderizer .... *5 gms/ 1 tsp*
Black cardamoms .... *2 gms / ½ tsp*	Mustard oil (*sarson ka tel*) .... *50 ml / 3¹/₃ tbs*
Black pepper .... *5 gms / 1 tsp*	Mustard seeds (*raee*) .... *5 gms / 1 tsp*
Chaat masala .... *5 gms / 1 tsp*	Onion seeds (*kalonji*) .... *5 gms / 1 tsp*
Cloves .... *3 gms /²/₃ tsp*	Raw papaya, a small piece pounded
Garlic paste .... *10 gms / 2 tsp*	Red chilli powder .... *15 gms / 1 tbs*
Ginger paste .... *10 gms / 2 tsp*	Salt to taste
Gram flour (*besan*) .... *10 gms / 2 tsp*	Yoghurt, whisked .... *50 gms / ¼ cup*

Method:

1. Flatten the chops with a steak hammer. Rub with papaya, ginger and garlic pastes, salt and keep aside.
2. Heat the gram flour in a pan till light brown and sprinkle over the lamb chops.
3. Add the remaining ingredients (except chaat masala and lemon juice) to the yoghurt and mix well. Marinate the chops in this mixture for 2 hours.
4. Preheat the oven to 175 °C (350 °F).
5. Skewer the chops and roast in a hot tandoor or oven until cooked, basting occasionally.

To Serve:

Remove the chops from the skewer. Sprinkle chaat masala and lemon juice and serve hot.

HYDERABADI KEEMA

The humble minced lamb transformed into a gourmet delight.

Serves: 4-5   **Preparation time:** 20 minutes   **Cooking time:** 20 minutes

INGREDIENTS:

Lamb, minced .... *1 kg*
Bay leaves (*tej patta*) *2*
Black pepper, crushed .... *6 gms / 1¹/₃ tsp*
Cinnamon sticks (4 cm pieces) *3*
Cloves *10*
Fresh mint leaves .... *10 gms / 2 tsp*
Garam masala .... *10 gms / 2 tsp*
Garlic paste .... *50 gms / 3¹/₃ tbs*
Ginger, finely julienned .... *6 gms / 1 tsp*
Ginger paste .... *50 gms / 3¹/₃ tbs*

Green coriander, chopped .... *15 gms / 1 tbs*
Green cardamoms *8*
Green chillies, slit in half *10*
Mace powder (*javitri*) .... *3 gms / ²/₃ tsp*
Onions, diced .... *25 gms / 5 tsp*
Red chilli powder .... *10 gms / 2 tsp*
Refined oil .... *100 ml / ½ cup*
Salt for seasoning
Yoghurt, whisked .... *100 gms / ½ cup*

METHOD:

1. Heat the oil in a pan, add bay leaves, cloves, cinnamon sticks and cardamoms, sauté over medium heat until they begin to crackle.
2. Add the diced onions and sauté until soft.
3. Add ginger and garlic pastes, red chilli powder and minced lamb, stir and cook until the raw smell of the ingredients disappears.
4. Add garam masala, crushed black pepper and yoghurt. Bring it to a slow boil, cover and simmer until the liquid evaporates.
5. Add salt and mace powder.

TO SERVE:

Serve hot, garnished with fresh mint leaves, green coriander, julienned ginger and slit green chillies, accompanied by a Raita (page 83) and any Indian bread.

33

CHAMP MASALA

Lamb chops in a spicy marinade.

Serves: 4-6   **Preparation time:** 30 minutes   **Cooking time:** 1 hour 15 minutes

INGREDIENTS:

Lamb chops .... *1 kg*	Garlic paste .... *10 gms / 2 tsp*
Almonds, blanched *12*	Ginger, chopped finely .... *10 gms / 2 tsp*
Brown sugar .... *5 gms / 1 tsp*	Green or Red chillies, deseeded and sliced *2*
Butter or oil .... *40 ml / 2²/₃ tbs*	Saffron (optional), few strands dissolved in 1 tsp milk
Cardamom seeds .... *3 gms / ½ tsp*	Onions (medium size), chopped *2*
Cayenne pepper .... *5 gms / 1 tsp*	Salt to taste
Cloves, whole .... *2 or 3*	Sesame (*til*) seeds .... *10 gms / 2 tsp*
Coriander leaves, chopped .... *10 gms / 2 tsp*	Yoghurt .... *175 ml / ¾ cup*
Cumin seeds .... *15 gms / 1 tbs*	

METHOD:

1. Blend cumin seeds, ginger, garlic paste, cardamom seeds, cloves, almonds, sesame seeds, cayenne pepper, sugar and 2 tbs yoghurt to a puree, adding more yoghurt if the mixture is dry. Pour mixture into a bowl and set aside.
2. Melt butter/oil in a large *kadhai* (wok) or pan. Add onions and fry till golden brown. Stir in the masala paste and fry for five minutes stirring constantly. Add a spoonful water at a time if the mixture becomes too dry.

Add the lamb chops and fry for 10 minutes on medium heat, turning chops frequently.
3. Beat the remaining yoghurt and saffron together, pour it into the lamb and mix well. Bring to a boil then reduce heat to very low, simmer for ½ hour.
4. Preheat oven to 150 °C (300 °F).
5. Transfer chops into a casserole and put into the oven to cook for at least 25 minutes.

TO SERVE:

Remove from the oven, garnish with
chopped coriander. Serve at once accompanied by
hot Naans (page 75) or Rotis (page 77).

Sabz Gosht

Lamb simmered in coconut milk. An exotic blend.

Serves: 4-6   **Preparation time**: 3-3½ hours   **Cooking time**: 1½ hours

Ingredients:

Lamb (leg or shoulder) .... *1 kg*
Almonds, blanched and cut into thin slivers *12*
Coconut milk .... *250 gms / 1¼ cup*
Fresh coriander, chopped .... *115 gms / 1 cup*
Garlic, ground .... *18 gms / 1¹/₃ tbs*
Ginger, ground .... *25 gms / 1²/₃ tbs*

Green chillies, whole *3*
Oil .... *175 ml / 1 cup*
Raisins, cut into halves .... *15 gms / 1 tbs*
Red chillies, whole *3*
Salt to taste
Yoghurt .... *400 gms / 2 cups*

Method:

1. Clean lamb and cut into pieces. Add ginger and garlic to the meat and marinade for 2 hours.
2. Heat oil, fry almonds and raisins separately to golden brown. Keep aside.
3. In the same oil, add the meat and fry till brown.
4. Mix in salt and yoghurt. Cook till the yoghurt dries up.

5. Stir in green and red chillies and chopped coriander.
6. Then add coconut milk and cook on low flame, stirring regularly without adding any water. When the lamb is tender, add almonds and raisins. Cover the pan and simmer till all the liquids have dried up.

To Serve:

Serve hot, accompanied by Naans (page 75)
or Chappatis (page 75).

Gosht Shahi Korma

Lamb curried with yoghurt, cream and almonds.

Serves: 4-5   **Preparation time:** 1 hour   **Cooking time:** 30 minutes

Ingredients:

Lamb (cut into boneless cubes) .... *1 kg*	Ginger paste .... *25 gms / 5 tsp*
Almond paste .... *50 gms / ¼ cup*	Green cardamoms *10*
Bay leaves (*tej patta*) *2*	Green cardamom powder .... *2 gms / ½ tsp*
Butter (unsalted) .... *100 gms / ½ cup*	Green chillies .... *50 gms / 6-10*
Cinnamon sticks *5*	Onions, sliced .... *150 gms / ¾ cup*
Clarified butter (*ghee*) .... *150 gms / ¾ cup*	Salt to taste
Cream .... *100 ml / ½ cup*	White pepper powder .... *2 gms / ½ tsp*
Garlic paste .... *25 gms / 5 tsp*	Yoghurt .... *250 gms / 1¼ cup*

Method:

1. Rub the ginger and garlic pastes over the lamb and keep aside for 1 hour.
2. Heat the clarified butter and butter. Fry bay leaves, cinnamon sticks and cardamoms till they crackle, then add onions and sauté till soft.
3. Add the cubed lamb and cook over high heat until the lamb changes colour.
4. Add yoghurt and almond paste and cook on low heat for another 25 minutes or until tender. Season to taste with cream, green chillies, white pepper powder, salt and green cardamom powder.

To Serve:

Serve hot, accompanied by Roti (page 77).

LAMB ROGAN JOSH

A mild Kashmiri lamb dish.

Serves: 4-5   **Preparation time:** 15 minutes   **Cooking time:** 35 minutes

INGREDIENTS:

Lamb (preferably chops) .... *1 kg*
Bay leaves (*tej patta*) *3*
Black cumin seeds (*shah jeera*) .... *2 gms / ½ tsp*
Cinnamon sticks *2*
Cloves *10*
Fennel seed powder (*saunf*) .... *5 gms / 1 tsp*
Ginger paste .... *10 gms / 2 tsp*
Green cardamoms *8*

Lamb stock / Water .... *200 ml / 1 cup*
Onions, chopped .... *180 gms / ¾ cup*
Red chilli powder .... *10 gms / 2 tsp*
Oil .... *60 ml / 4 tbs*
Salt to taste
Sugar .... *5 gms / 1 tsp*
Tomatoes, skinned, deseeded
and chopped .... *400 gms / 2 cups*

METHOD:

1. Remove excess fat, pat with a paper towel, sprinkle with salt and keep aside for 10 minutes.
2. Heat oil, add sugar, cloves, bay leaves, green cardamoms and cinnamon sticks and sauté for 2-3 minutes.
3. Add the lamb chops and cook over medium heat until they are lightly browned.
4. Add the chopped onions and sauté till browned.

5. Add red chilli powder, black cumin seeds, chopped tomatoes and ginger paste, fry till oil separates from the gravy.
6. Add the stock/water and cook until the chops are tender. Stir in fennel seed powder. Cover and simmer for 10 minutes on a low fire.

TO SERVE:

Serve hot, garnished with a pinch of fennel seed powder, accompanied by steamed rice or Roti (page 77).

CHUTNEY FISH TIKKA

Grilled fish in a tangy marinade.

Serves: 4-6   **Preparation time:** 3½ hours   **Cooking time:** 15 minutes

INGREDIENTS:

Fish fillets, cleaned and cut into cubes .... *1 kg*
Butter/oil for basting
Carom (*ajwain*) seeds .... *8 gms / 1½ tsp*
Cream .... *45 ml / 3 tbs*
Cumin (*jeera*) powder .... *10 gms / 2 tsp*
Garam masala .... *15 gms / 1 tbs*
Garlic paste .... *20 gms / 4 tsp*

Gram flour/Rice flour .... *20 gms / 4 tsp*
Lemon juice .... *30 ml / 2 tbs*
*Mint or coriander chutney .... *134 ml / ²/₃ cup*
Salt to taste
White pepper powder .... *2½ gms / ½ tsp*
Yoghurt, drained .... *60 gms / 4 tbs*

METHOD:

* For Mint chutney turn to page 83
1. Mix yoghurt with cream, garlic paste, carom seeds, white pepper, cumin powder, garam masala, salt, lemon juice, mint/coriander chutney and gram/rice flour.
2. Add fish cubes to the marinade, coat evenly and set aside for 2-3 hrs.
3. Skewer fish 2 cms apart and roast in a pre-heated oven 175 °C (350 °F) or a tandoor for 8-10 minutes. Baste with butter once before roasting is complete.

TO SERVE:

Garnish with onion rings and serve hot.

TANDOORI POMFRET

An entire fish tendered spicy with a marinade.

Serves: 4　　　　**Preparation time:** 2½ hours　　　　**Cooking time:** 15 minutes

INGREDIENTS:

Pomfret (450 gms each) 4	Lemon juice .... *30 ml / 2 tbs*
Carom (*ajwain*) seeds .... *10 gms / 2 tsp*	Oil for brushing
Cream .... *45 ml / 3 tbs*	Red chilli powder .... *10 gms / 2 tsp*
Cumin (*jeera*) powder .... *10 gms / 2 tsp*	Salt to taste
Garlic paste .... *15 gms / 1 tbs*	Turmeric powder .... *5 gms / 1 tsp*
Ginger paste .... *15 gms / 1 tbs*	White pepper powder .... *3 gms / ½ tsp*
Gram flour (*besan*) .... *30 gms / 2 tbs*	Yoghurt, drained .... *60 gms / 4 tbs*

METHOD:

1. Mix yoghurt with cream, ginger and garlic paste, carom seeds, gram flour, white pepper powder, salt, red chilli, cumin powder, lemon juice and turmeric.
2. Rub mixture on both sides of the fish, set aside for 2 hours.
3. Preheat oven to 175 °C (350 °F).
4. Skewer fish from mouth to tail and roast for 10 minutes. Hang skewers to let excess moisture drip.
5. Brush or baste with oil and roast again for 5 minutes or until done.

TO SERVE:

Remove to a platter, garnish with onion rings and serve hot, accompanied by Mint chutney (page 83).

TANDOORI PRAWNS

Juicy prawns roasted in a tangy marinade.

Serves: 4   **Preparation time:** 2 hours   **Cooking time:** 15 minutes

INGREDIENTS:

Prawns (king size)	12	
Butter for basting		
Carom (*ajwain*) seeds	*5 gms / 1 tsp*	
Chick-pea flour	*45 gms / 3 tbs*	
Chaat masala	*5 gms / 1 tsp*	
Garam masala	*5 gms / 1 tsp*	
Garlic paste	*45 gms / 3 tbs*	
Ginger paste	*45 gms / 3 tbs*	
Lemon juice	*75 ml / 5 tbs*	
Salt to taste		
Turmeric powder	*2½ gms / ½ tsp*	
Yellow chilli powder	*5 gms / 1 tsp*	
Yoghurt	*480 ml / 2¹/₃ cups*	

METHOD:

1. Reserve 2 tablespoons lemon juice and mix the rest with the ginger and garlic pastes.
2. Add salt, chick-pea flour, carom seeds, yoghurt, yellow chilli powder, garam masala and turmeric. Marinade the prawns in this for 2 hours.
3. Arrange on skewers and cook in a tandoor till half done, about 5-7 minutes.
4. Remove and set aside for 10 minutes. Cook again in the tandoor for 2 minutes.
5. Baste with butter and replace in the tandoor for approximately 3 more minutes.
6. Remove from skewers and arrange on a platter. Sprinkle with chaat masala and the reserved lemon juice.

TO SERVE:

Serve hot, accompanied by a green salad.

FRIED FISH

Deep fried fish fillets.

Serves: 4   **Prep. time:** 1 hr   **Cooking time:** 20 mins

INGREDIENTS:

Fish fillets	8
Juice of lemons	2
Oil for deep frying	
Salt and Pepper to taste	

For the Batter:

Water	*125 ml / ½ cup*
Gram flour (*besan*)	*75 gms / 5 tbs*
Red chilli powder	*5 gms / 1 tsp*
Rice flour	*25 gms / 5 tsp*
Turmeric powder	*5 gms / 1 tsp*

METHOD:

1. Rub each fillet with salt and pepper all over. Put in a large bowl and sprinkle lemon juice. Set aside to marinate for at least 1 hour.
2. Sift the gramflour, rice flour, turmeric and chilli powder into a bowl. Stir in the water and mix to form a smooth batter.
3. Remove fish from the marinade and pat dry.
4. Fill *kadhai* (wok) or frying pan with oil and heat till it is smoking. Dip each fish fillet in the batter and fry for 5 minutes or until they are golden brown on both sides. Remove from oil and drain on kitchen towels.

TO SERVE:

Serve hot, garnished with onion rings.

TOMATO FISH

Fish fillets in tomato curry, a gourmet's delight.

Serves: 4 **Prep. time:** 30 mins **Cooking time:** 20-25 mins

INGREDIENTS:

Fish fillets (firm and white), deboned and cubed	*1 kg*
Coriander, ground	*15 gms / 1 tbs*
Garam masala	*10 gms / 2 tsp*
Green chillies, slit in half, deseeded	*4*
Lemon juice	*15 gms / 1 tbs*
Oil	*50 ml / ¼ cup*
Onions (medium), sliced	*2*
Red chilli powder	*5 gms / 1 tsp*
Salt to taste	
Sour cream	*30 gms / 2 tbs*
Sugar	*5 gms / 1 tsp*
Tomatoes, blanched, deseeded and chopped	*½ kg*
Turmeric powder	*10 gms / 2 tsp*

METHOD:

1. Rub 1½ tsp of turmeric and salt into the fish cubes and set aside.
2. Heat oil in a deep pan, fry the fish cubes until they are evenly browned. Put aside on a plate.
3. Add onions and sauté. Stir in chilli powder, sugar, garam masala, coriander powder and the remaining turmeric. Cook for 2 min. Add tomatoes, sour cream, lemon juice, green chillies, bring to a boil, stirring continuously.
4. Add fried fish cubes to the sauce and coat evenly. Simmer for 10 minutes or until fish flakes easily.

TO SERVE:

Serve hot, accompanied by any Indian Roti (page 77).

TANDOORI LOBSTER

A spectacular party special!

Serves: 4-5   **Preparation time:** 5 hours   **Cooking time:** 10 minutes

INGREDIENTS:

Lobster (medium) 4	Gram flour (*besan*) .... *50 gms / 3¹/₃ tbs*
Butter for basting .... *100 gms / ½ cup*	Mustard oil (*sarson ka tel*) .... *50 ml / 4 tbs*
Carom seeds (*ajwain*) .... *3 gms /²/₃ tsp*	Red chilli paste .... *5 gms / 1 tsp*
Cottage cheese (**paneer*) .... *50 gms / ¼ cup*	Salt to taste
Egg *1*	Vinegar, malt .... *120 ml /²/₃ cup*
Garam masala .... *10 gms / 2 tsp*	White pepper powder .... *5 gms / 1 tsp*
Garlic paste .... *20 gms / 4 tsp*	Yoghurt, drained .... *200 gms / 1 cup*
Ginger paste .... *20 gms / 4 tsp*	

METHOD:

* For recipe of paneer see page 57

1. Cut each lobster shell into half, then shell and devein the lobster. Wash and dry the shells, dip them in hot oil drain and keep aside.
2. Marinate the lobsters in a mixture made of ginger and garlic pastes, carom seeds, vinegar and salt. Keep aside for 1 hour.
3. Whisk yoghurt in a large bowl, add the remaining ingredients and coat the lobsters with this mixture. Keep aside for 3 hours.
4. Skewer the lobsters 2 cm apart. Keep a tray underneath to collect the excess drippings.
5. Roast in a moderately hot tandoor or pre-heated oven of 175 ˚C (350 ˚F) for 5 minutes.
6. Baste with butter and cook again for 2 minutes.

TO SERVE:

Place the lobster on the shell, garnish with lettuce, tomato slices and onion rings. Serve hot.

Prawn Til Tikka

Fried prawns flavoured with sesame.

Serves: 4-6   **Preparation time:** 45 minutes   **Cooking time:** 15 minutes

INGREDIENTS:

King Prawns 12	Oil .... *220 ml / 1¼ cup*
Chilli powder .... *3 gms / ½ tsp*	Paprika .... *5 gms / 1 tsp*
Coriander, chopped (optional) .... *5 gms / 1 tsp*	Sesame (*til*) seeds .... *30 gms / 2 tbs*
Garlic, crushed .... *5 gms / 1 tsp*	Turmeric powder .... *3 gms / ½ tsp*
Lemon juice .... *10 gms / 2 tsp*	Salt to taste

METHOD:

1. Wash, clean and devein prawns. Pat them dry. Rub lemon juice into the prawns. Set aside.
2. Coarsely grind 1 tsp sesame seeds. Put the rest aside to be used later for frying.
3. Mix the coarsely ground sesame seeds alongwith 1 tsp oil and the rest of the ingredients to form a marinade. Coat the prawns in this marinade, cover the dish and put aside for 30 minutes.
4. Heat oil in a frying pan till it is smoking hot. Reduce fire to medium. Coat prawns evenly with remaining sesame seeds and deep fry till they are crisp and golden brown.

TO SERVE:

Garnish with chopped coriander and lemon wedges
and serve hot, accompanied by chilli sauce.

GOAN FISH CURRY

*This traditional spicy fish curry comes from Goa
and is a must in every Goan meal.*

Serves: 4   **Preparation time:** 1 hour   **Cooking time:** 30 minutes

INGREDIENTS:

Pomfret darnes .... 600 gms	Lemon juice .... 60 ml / 4 tbs
Coconut, grated .... 160 gms / ²/₃ cup	Onions, chopped .... 60 gms / ¼ cup
Coconut milk .... 160 ml / ²/₃ cup	Red chillies, whole 15
Coriander seeds .... 15 gms / 1 tbs	Salt to taste
Cumin (*jeera*) seeds .... 5 gms / 1 tsp	Tamarind (*imlee*), deseeded .... 45 gms / 3 tbs
Garlic paste .... 5 gms / 1 tsp	Tomatoes, chopped .... 60 gms / ¼ cup
Ginger paste .... 20 gms / 4 tsp	Turmeric powder .... 5 gms / 1 tsp
Green chillies 4	Water .... 240 ml / 1¼ cup
Groundnut oil .... 60 ml / 4 tbs	

METHOD:

1. Sprinkle salt and lemon on the fish, marinade for an hour.
2. Blend the coconut, whole chillies, cumin seeds, coriander seeds, turmeric, tamarind and the ginger and garlic pastes together with the coconut milk.
3. Heat oil in a *kadhai* (wok). Add the onions and sauté till golden brown. Add tomatoes and cook for 3 to 4 minutes or until the tomatoes are mashed.
4. Add the blended mixture and water, bring to a boil. Mix in green chillies and the fish, simmer for 7 minutes. Bring to a boil and then let simmer for 2 minutes. Do not cover the pot at any stage while the curry is being cooked.

TO SERVE:

Remove to a bowl and serve hot,
accompanied by boiled rice.

PRAWN CURRY

Prawns in a delectable coconut curry.

Serves: 4   **Preparation time:** 45 minutes   **Cooking time:** 35 minutes

INGREDIENTS:

Prawns, cleaned and deveined .... *1 kg*	Lemon juice .... *5 gms / 1 tsp*
Beef or Chicken stock .... *150 ml / ¾ cup*	Oil .... *100 ml / ½ cup*
Cinnamon, ground .... *5 gms / 1 tsp*	Onion, finely chopped *1*
Cloves, ground .... *5 gms / 1 tsp*	Red chilli powder .... *10 gms / 2 tsp*
Creamed coconut .... *100 gms / ½ cup*	Salt to taste
Flour .... *5 gms / 1 tsp*	Sugar .... *5 gms / 1 tsp*
Garlic, crushed .... *5 gms / 1 tsp*	Turmeric powder .... *5 gms / 1 tsp*

METHOD:

1. Heat oil in a saucepan, sauté chopped onion, garlic paste and ground cloves. Fry lightly, add flour, turmeric, chilli, sugar and cinnamon. Cook gently for a few minutes.
2. Gradually add stock and creamed coconut to the pan and bring to boil stirring constantly. Reduce heat and simmer for 10 minutes.
3. Add the prawns and lemon juice. Season with salt, cook for another ten minutes.

TO SERVE:

Serve hot, accompanied by any Indian bread.

PANEER SEEKH KEBAB

Vegetarian, skewered kebabs.

Serves: 4-5   **Preparation time:** 15 minutes   **Cooking time:** 15 minutes

INGREDIENTS:

Cottage cheese (*paneer*), grated fine .... *1 kg*	Lemon juice .... *15 ml / 1 tbs*
Butter for basting .... *20 gms / 4 tsp*	Onions, grated .... *150 gms / ¾ cup*
Cornflour .... *15 gms / 1 tbs*	Red chilli powder .... *5 gms / 1 tsp*
Garam masala .... *10 gms / 2 tsp*	Salt for seasoning
Ginger paste .... *25 gms / 5 tsp*	White pepper powder .... *5 gms / 1 tsp*
Green chillies, chopped *6*	

METHOD:

* **Recipe for Paneer:** Put 3 litres milk to boil. Just before it boils add 90 ml/6 tbs lemon juice or vinegar. Milk will curdle as it comes to boil. Strain through a muslin cloth, allowing all whey and moisture to drain. Still wrapped in the muslin, place paneer under a weight for 2-3 hours to allow to set into a block which can be cut into cubes or grated.

1. Mix all the ingredients, adding the cornflour in the end.
2. Divide this mixture into 15 equal balls.
3. Preheat the oven to 150-75 ̊C (300-50 ̊F).
4. Skewer each ball. Spread by pressing each along the length of the skewer with a wet hand, making each kebab about 8-10 cms long, 1 cm apart.
5. Roast in oven/tandoor/charcoal grill for 5-6 minutes, baste with melted butter and roast for another 2 minutes. Remove from skewers.

TO SERVE:

Garnish with slices of cucumber, tomato, onion and serve hot, accompanied by Mint chutney (page 83).

TANDOORI CAPSICUM

These stuffed and grilled peppers are delightfully different.

Serves: 4   **Preparation time:** 15-20 minutes   **Cooking time:** 15 minutes

INGREDIENTS:

Capsicum, medium sized	250 gms / 4 pieces
Cabbage, shredded	120 gms / ½ cup
Cashewnuts, broken	5 gms / 1 tsp
Coriander leaves, chopped	5 gms / 1 tsp
Carrots, grated	80 gms / 1/3 cup
Cottage cheese (*paneer*), grated	240 gms / 1¼ cup
Cumin (*jeera*) seeds	2½ gms / ½ tsp
French beans, thinly sliced	60 gms / ¼ cup
Garam masala	a pinch
Garlic paste	2½ gms / ½ tsp
Ginger paste	2½ gms / ½ tsp
Green peas	20 gms / 4 tsp
Oil	15 ml / 1 tbs
Raisins	5 gms / 1 tsp
Red chilli powder	2½ gms / ½ tsp
Salt to taste	

METHOD:

* For recipe of paneer see page 57

1. Slice the capsicums at the stem end, scoop out the seeds and save the stem end.
2. Heat oil. Add cumin and let it splutter. Add ginger and garlic pastes and sauté for a few minutes.
3. Add all vegetables and stir fry. Season with salt and red chilli powder.
4. Fry till the oil surfaces. Take off from fire.
5. Add grated cottage cheese and garam masala.
6. Cool mixture. Add cashewnuts, raisins and coriander.
7. Stuff the capsicums with the mixture. Cover with stem end and secure with toothpicks.
8. Skewer the capsicums and grill for 5 minutes or bake in a tandoor for 8 minutes.

TO SERVE:

Remove the toothpicks, put on a platter and garnish with lemon wedges, onion rings and tomato slices. Serve hot.

PALAK BHAJEE

Stir fried Spinach with garlic and turmeric.

Serves: 4-5 **Prep. time:** 10 min **Cooking time:** 15 min

INGREDIENTS:

Spinach (*palak*), fresh or frozen	1 kg
Asafoetida (*heeng*)	a pinch
Garlic, peeled, cut lengthwise	60 gms / 4 tbs
Oil	60 ml / 4 tbs
Onions, sliced or chopped	100 gms / ½ cup
Red chillies, dried, cut in half	8
Red chilli powder	5 gms / 1 tsp
Salt to taste	
Turmeric powder	3 gms / ⅔ tsp

METHOD:

1. Wash the spinach leaves and chop roughly.
2. Heat the oil in a *kadhai* (wok) to smoking point. Reduce the heat, add the dry red chillies, onions, garlic, red chilli powder, turmeric powder and asafoetida and stir fry for 2-3 minutes.
3. Immediately add the spinach leaves, toss and stir fry.
4. Sprinkle with salt, cover and cook on very low heat for 6-7 minutes.

TO SERVE:

Serve hot, accompanied by Daal (page 68) and Rotis (page 77).

BRINJAL BHARTA

A traditionally cooked Aubergine delight.

Serves: 4 **Prep. time:** 10 min **Cooking time:** 45 min

INGREDIENTS:

Aubergine (approx ½ kg)	1
Coriander leaves	5 gms / 1 tsp
Cumin seeds	1½ gms / ¼ tsp
Garam masala	5 gms / 1 tsp
Garlic, crushed	5 gms / 1 tsp
Green chillies, sliced	2
Oil or ghee	30 ml / 2 tbs
Salt to taste	
Spring onions/ordinary onions (minced)	3
Yoghurt	200 gms / 1 cup

METHOD:

1. Cut aubergine lengthwise into half. Cover with foil and bake in a moderately hot oven (175 °C/350 °F) for 40 minutes or until tender. Remove skin and mash the flesh of the aubergine.
2. Heat oil, add cumin seeds and fry until dark brown in colour. Add minced onions and fry until golden brown.
3. Add garlic, green chillies, aubergine, cook on low flame for 15-20 minutes.
4. Add salt and yoghurt, cook on medium heat for another 5-8 minutes stirring occasionally. Add garam masala and chopped coriander.

TO SERVE:

Serve hot, accompanied by Chappatis (see page 75).

VEGETABLE KORMA

Mixed vegetables in a creamy gravy, a nourishing meal in itself.

Serves: 4-6   **Preparation time:** 20 minutes   **Cooking time:** 15 minutes

INGREDIENTS:

Cottage cheese (*paneer*), cubed .... *100 gms / ½ cup*
Boiled vegetables (Carrots, French beans,
Peas, Potatoes) .... *400 gms / 2 cups*
Clarified butter (*ghee*) or oil .... *100 ml / ½ cup*
Coriander powder .... *10 gms / 2 tsp*
Fresh cream .... *100 gms / ½ cup*
Garam masala .... *5 gms / 1 tsp*
Garlic paste .... *5 gms / 1 tsp*

Ginger paste .... *5 gms / 1 tsp*
Milk .... *200 gms / 1 cup*
Onions, chopped *2*
Red chilli powder .... *5 gms / 1 tsp*
Salt to taste
Tomatoes, chopped *3*
Turmeric powder .... *3 gms / ½ tsp*

METHOD:

*** Recipe for Paneer:** Put 3 litres milk to boil. Just before it boils add 90 ml/6 tbs lemon juice or vinegar. Milk will curdle as it comes to boil. Strain through a muslin cloth, allowing all whey and moisture to drain. Still wrapped in the muslin, place paneer under a weight for 2-3 hours to allow to set into a block which can be cut into cubes.

1. Heat oil till smoking hot and fry paneer cubes till light brown in colour. Set aside.
2. In the same oil, add chopped onions and sauté. Add ginger and garlic pastes, sauté further for 1 minute.
3. Stir in chopped tomatoes, turmeric powder, red chilli powder, coriander powder, garam masala and salt. Cook on medium heat for at least 5 minutes, stirring continuously.
4. Add mixed vegetables, fried paneer cubes, milk and cream and cook further for 3-5 minutes till the vegetables and paneer cubes are tender to touch.

TO SERVE:

Serve hot, accompanied by Chappatis (page 75)
or Rotis (page 77).

Kadhai Paneer

Cottage cheese fingers cooked in a kadhai. A chilli hot, semi-dry and colourful curry!

Serves: 4   **Preparation time:** 15 minutes   **Cooking time:** 10 minutes

Ingredients:

Cottage cheese (*paneer*) .... 600 gms
Black pepper .... 8 gms / 1²/₃ tsp
Capsicum .... 40 gms / 2²/₃ tbs
Coriander leaves, chopped .... 15 gms / 1 tbs
Coriander powder .... 10 gms / 2 tsp
Coriander seeds... 10 gms / 2 tsp
Fenugreek powder (*methi*) .... 5 gms / 1 tsp

Garam masala .... 8 gms / 1²/₃ tsp
Ginger, julienned .... 15 gms / 1 tbs
Oil.. 40 ml / 2²/₃ tbs
Onions, chopped .... 40 gms / 2²/₃ tbs
Red chillies, whole 15
Salt to taste
Tomato purée .... 150 ml / ¾ cup

Method:

* For recipe of paneer see page 61

1. Cut the paneer into fingers. Cut the capsicum into halves, deseed and make juliennes or cut into small, even squares.
2. Pound the red chillies and coriander seeds with a pestle to a powder.
3. Heat the oil in a *kadhai* (wok), sauté the onions and capsicum over medium heat for 2 minutes.
4. Add the pounded spices and two-thirds of the ginger, stir for 1 minute.
5. Add the tomato purée and salt, bring to a boil, simmer until the oil separates from the gravy.
6. Add the paneer and stir gently for 2-3 minutes.
7. Stir in fenugreek powder, garam masala, coriander powder and black pepper.

> ## To Serve:
>
> Garnish with chopped coriander leaves and the remaining julienned ginger. Serve hot, accompanied by Roti (page 77) or Parantha (page 76) and Salad or Raita (page 83).

CRUNCHY OKRA

Crispy fried Okra.

Serves: 4-6　　　　　　**Preparation time:** 40 minutes　　　　　　**Cooking time:** 30 minutes

INGREDIENTS:

Okra (*bhindi*)	½ kg	Green chillies, sliced (optional)	2
Carom seeds (*ajwain*)	*2 gms / ¼ tsp*	Oil for frying	
Chaat masala	*3 gms / ½ tsp*	Raw mango powder (*amchoor*)	*3 gms / ½ tsp*
Garam masala	*5 gms / 1 tsp*	Red chillies	*5 gms / 1 tsp*
Ginger, julienned	*7 gms / 1½ tsp*	Salt to taste	
Gram flour (*besan*)	*45 gms / 3 tbs*		

METHOD:

1. Snip off both ends of each okra, slice lengthwise into four slices.
2. Spread all sliced okra on a flat dish and sprinkle evenly with salt, chilli powder, garam masala, mango powder and chaat masala. Mix gently to coat okra evenly.
3. Now sprinkle gram flour over the okra and mix in so they are coated evenly, without adding any water preferably.
4. Divide the okra into two portions. Heat oil in a *kadhai* (wok) or a pan till it is smoking. Fry one portion coated okra slices, separating each lightly with a fork. Do not allow slices to stick to each other.
5. Remove from oil when both sides are crispy and brown in colour. Fry the other portion in the same way and serve at once.

TO SERVE:

Garnish with julienned ginger and green chillies
and serve hot, accompanied by Chappatis (page 75).

Mushroom Masala

A curry for the mushroom lovers.

Serves: 4   **Preparation time:** 10 minutes   **Cooking time:** 20 minutes

Ingredients:

Mushrooms .... ½ kg	Onions, sliced 2
Coriander leaves, chopped .... 15 gms / 1 tbs	Red chilli powder .... 3 gms/ ½ tsp
Garam masala .... 3 gms / ½ tsp	Salt to taste
Garlic paste .... 5 gms / 1 tsp	Tomato, chopped 1
Oil .... 22 ml / 4½ tsp	Turmeric powder .... 3 gms / ½ tsp

Method:

1. Cut mushrooms in slices.
2. Heat oil and fry onions until golden in colour. Add garlic paste and chopped tomatoes, mix well.
3. Put in turmeric, garam masala, chilli powder, salt and fry for 3-4 mins. Stir in mushrooms and simmer until mushrooms are tender, adding very little water if necessary.

To Serve:

Garnish with coriander and serve hot.

DAAL MAKHANI

*Black lentils cooked over a slow fire. A favourite
with almost all gourmets.*

Serves: 4   **Prep. time:** 6-7 hrs   **Cooking time:** 3 hrs

INGREDIENTS:

Black lentils, whole (*black urad daal*) .... *300 gms / 1½ cups*
Butter .... *120 ml / ½ cup*
Chilli powder .... *5 gms / 1 tsp*
Coriander leaves .... *10 gms / 2 tsp*
Cream .... *160 ml / ²/₃ cup*
Garlic paste .... *20 gms / 4 tsp*
Ginger paste .... *20 gms / 4 tsp*
Green chillies, sliced *2*
Salt to taste
Tomato purée .... *160 ml / ²/₃ cup*

METHOD:

1. Soak lentils for at least 3 hrs; best soaked overnight.
2. Add 1.5 litres water to the lentils and cook over a
   low flame till grain splits.
3. Stir the lentils to mash them. Set aside.
4. Heat butter, fry ginger and garlic pastes. Add green
   chillies, tomato puree, salt and chilli powder. Cook for
   2-3 minutes, add the boiled lentils. Cook further for
   10-15 minutes, stirring occasionally.
5. Add chopped coriander and cream (leaving 1 tbs aside).

TO SERVE:

Serve hot, garnished with the reserved cream and
accompanied by Naan (page 75)/Tandoori roti (page 77).

ALU MATTAR

Curried potatoes and peas.

Serves: 4   **Prep. time:** 30 min   **Cooking time:** 45 min

INGREDIENTS:

Potatoes, peeled and cubed .... *225 gms*
Peas, frozen or fresh .... *½ kg*
Coriander, chopped .... *30 gms / 2 tbs*
Garlic cloves .... *3-5 gms / ½ tsp*
Ginger, peeled, finely chopped .... *8 gms / 1½ tsp*
Green chilli, chopped *1*
Oil or *ghee* .... *30 ml / 2 tbs*
Onion (medium), finely chopped *1*
Tomatoes (medium), chopped *2*
Turmeric powder .... *5 gms / 1 tsp*
Water .... *100 ml / ½ cup*

METHOD:

1. Heat oil or *ghee* in a pan. Add onions and sauté, stir in
   ginger, garlic and green chilli. Cook for 5 minutes stirring
   continuously.
2. Add the chopped tomatoes and cook for 2-3 mins until
   tomatoes are soft.
3. Stir in the turmeric powder, peas, potatoes and salt.
   Cover the pan and simmer for 20 mins.
4. Add half cup of water to prevent the mixture from
   becoming too dry.
5. Stir in coriander leaves and simmer for another
   10-15 mins or until the vegetables are tender.

TO SERVE:

Serve at once accompanied by Chappatis (page 75)
or Pooris (page 76).

Punjabi Chana Masala

Bengal gram curry.

Serves: 4-5   **Preparation time:** 45 minutes   **Cooking time:** 1 hour

Ingredients:

Bengal gram (*chana*), split	*250 gms / 1¼ cups*
Bay leaf (*tej patta*)	*1*
Butter	*40 gms / 2²/₃ tbs*
Cinnamon stick	*1*
Garam masala	*6 gms / 1¹/₃ tsp*
Garlic paste	*10 gms / 2 tsp*
Ginger paste	*10 gms / 2 tsp*
Green coriander, chopped	*5 gms / 1 tsp*
Onions, chopped	*100 gms / ½ cup*
Tomatoes, skinned and chopped	*60 gms / 4 tbs*
Water	*1½ litres / 7½ cups*
Salt to taste	

Method:

1. Clean and wash the gram, soak for 30 minutes in a bowl of water.
2. Boil water in a saucepan. Add the bay leaf, cinnamon stick and the drained gram. Bring to a slow boil. Remove the scum from the top of the pan and simmer until gram is completely cooked and tender. Discard the bay leaf and cinnamon sticks from the gram.
3. Heat butter in a large saucepan and sauté onions till they are soft and golden. Add garam masala, ginger and garlic pastes, sauté over medium heat for 2-3 minutes.
4. Add tomatoes, cooked gram and salt to the saucepan, cover and cook for another 2-3 minutes.

To Serve:

Serve hot, garnished with green coriander, accompanied by Pooris (page 76).

LAMB BIRYANI

A Mughlai rice and meat dish. A meal in itself,
it can be served with only yoghurt as an accompaniment.

Serves: 4   **Preparation time:** 30 minutes   **Cooking time:** 1½ hours

INGREDIENTS:

Lamb (cut into 1" cubes)	*1 kg*	Ginger, julienned	*5 gms / 1 tsp*
Basmati rice	*400 gms / 2 cups*	Lamb stock	*400 ml / 2 cups*
Butter, melted	*45 gms / 3 tbs*	Mace (*javitri*) powder	*a pinch*
Cardamoms	*5*	Mint leaves, chopped	*5 gms / 1 tsp*
Cinnamon stick (1")	*1*	Onions, chopped	*120 gms / ½ cup*
Cloves	*2*	Saffron	*a pinch*
Cooking oil	*105 ml / 7 tbs*	Salt to taste	
Cream	*120 ml / ½ cup*	Vetivier (*kewda*)	*a few drops*
Dough to seal dish		Yellow chilli powder	*5 gms / 1 tsp*
Ginger, chopped	*30 gms / 2 tbs*	Yoghurt	*120 gms / ½ cup*

METHOD:

1. Heat oil in a pan and sauté chopped onions. Add cardamoms, cloves and cinnamon in the oil till they crackle, then add lamb pieces and sauté.
2. Add yoghurt, yellow chilli powder and salt. Stir till dry. Add stock and cook till meat is almost done.
3. In a separate pan boil rice in plenty of water, till the grains lengthen but are not fully cooked. Drain the water.
4. Remove meat pieces from curry and spread in a heat-proof casserole. Strain curry. Reserve half and pour the remainder onto the meat. Sprinkle mace, mint, chopped ginger, vetivier and half the cream over the meat.
5. Place half the rice on the meat pieces. Sprinkle reserved cream, the reserved liquid, melted butter and saffron, crushed in a spoonful of water over it.
6. Place rest of the rice on top. Cover and seal lid with dough. Cook over very gentle heat for about 10-15 minutes.

TO SERVE:

Serve hot, accompanied by Raita (page 83)
Note: Substitute lamb with chicken for **Chicken Biryani.**

JACKFRUIT PULAO

A delightful blend of rice with jackfruit.

Serves: 4-5   **Preparation time:** 45 minutes   **Cooking time:** 30 minutes

INGREDIENTS:

Rice, (Basmati or any long grain variety) .... *200 gms / 1 cup*
Jackfruit (cleaned, and cubed) .... *250 gms / 1½ cup*
Bay leaf (*tej patta*) *1*
Black cardamoms *2*
Black cumin (*shah jeera*) .... *5 gms / 1 tsp*
Cinnamon stick (medium) *1*
Cloves *4*
Ginger paste .... *10 gms / 2 tsp*
Oil .... *200 ml / 1 cup*
Onions, chopped .... *50 gms / ¼ cup*
Red chilli powder .... *3 gms / ½ tsp*
Salt to taste
Water .... *500 ml / 2½ cups*

White pepper powder .... *2 gms / ½ tsp*

For the garnishing:

Cashewnuts, sliced and fried .... *5 gms / 1 tsp*
Coriander, chopped .... *2 gms / ½ tsp*
Cream .... *30 ml / 2 tbs*
Ginger, julienned .... *3 gms / ½ tsp*
Green chillies, sliced and deseeded .... *5 gms/ 1 tsp*
Lemon juice .... *15 ml / 1 tbs*
Mace power (*javitri*) .... *2 gms / ½ tsp*
Onion, sliced and fried *1*

METHOD:

1. Clean, wash and soak the rice for at least 30 minutes.
2. Heat oil in a *kadhai* (wok) or a pan till it smoking. Fry jackfruit cubes till light brown in colour. Drain oil from them and keep aside.
3. Reheat same oil in a heavy pan, add the cloves, cinnamon stick, bay leaf, cardamom and cumin seeds, saute over medium heat until they begin to crackle.
4. Add chopped onions and sauté. Stir in the ginger paste and red chilli powder. Add the fried jackfruit, white pepper and salt. Cook for 3-4 minutes.
5. Stir in the water. Drain the rice and add to the pan. Bring to a boil, lower heat and cover the pan. Let it cook on low heat till the rice is done.
6. Remove lid and sprinkle with julienned ginger, slit green chillies, fried onions, mace powder, lemon juice, fried cashewnut, green coriander and cream.
7. Seal lid with dough, cook on very low heat for 10-15 minutes.

TO SERVE:

Serve hot, accompanied by Raita (page 83).
Note: For **Vegetable Pulao** substitute jackfruit with any mixed vegetable and follow the same method.

NAAN

Leavened bread.

Serves: 4-5   **Prep. time:** 3 hrs   **Cooking time:** 20 min

INGREDIENTS:

Flour .... *500 gms / 2½ cups*
Baking powder .... *5 gms / 1 tsp*
Baking soda .... *1 gm / ¼ tsp*
Clarified butter (*ghee*)/oil .... *25 ml / 5 tsp*
Egg *1*
Melon seeds .... *5 gms / 1 tsp*
Milk .... *50 ml / 3¹/₃ tbs*
Onion seeds (*kalonji*) .... *3 gms /²/₃ tsp*
Salt to taste
Sugar .... *10 gms / 2 tsp*

METHOD:

1. Sieve the flour, salt, baking soda and baking powder into a bowl. Add enough water to make a hard dough.
2. Whisk egg, sugar and milk in a bowl and knead into the dough to make it soft and smooth. Cover with moist cloth, keep aside for 10 minutes.
3. Add oil, knead and punch the dough, cover again with moist cloth, keep aside for 2 hrs to allow the dough to rise.
4. Heat the oven till moderately hot—175 °C (350 °F).
5. Divide the dough into 6 balls and place on a lightly floured surface. Sprinkle onion and melon seeds, flatten the balls slightly, cover and keep aside for 5 minutes.
6. Flatten each ball between the palms to make a round disc, then stretch on one side to form an elongated oval.
7. Place on a greased baking tray and bake for 2-3 min.

TO SERVE:

Serve hot, as an accompaniment to any curry dish.

CHAPPATIS

Wheat flour bread.

Serves: 4-6   **Prep. time:** ½ hr   **Cooking time:** ½ hr

INGREDIENTS:

Whole wheat flour .... *225 gms / 2 cups*
Clarified butter .... *15 ml / 1 tbs*
Salt (optional) .... *3 gms / ½ tsp*
Water .... *150 ml / ¾ cup*

METHOD:

1. Sieve flour and salt into a bowl. Make a well in the centre and pour in almost all water. Mix with your fingers and add rest of the water. Knead the dough for 5-8 mins or until it becomes smooth and elastic.
2. Put dough in a bowl, cover and keep aside for 20 mins at room temperature.
3. Turn out on to a floured board. Divide the dough into 8 portions. Roll out each portion into a thin round shape, about the size of a snack plate.
4. Heat a *tawa* (griddle) over moderate heat. Put one portion of rolled out dough on the pan. Cook until small spots appear on the surface. Then turn it over to the other side and cook for one minute.
5. Turn once again to the cooked side and roast it till it is of pale golden colour on both sides. Brush lightly with butter.

TO SERVE:

Serve hot, as an accompaniment to any curry dish.

LACHHA PARANTHA

A multi-layered bread, flavoured with fennel.

Serves: 4   **Prep. time:** 1½ hrs   **Cooking time:** 30 min

INGREDIENTS:

Flour .... *480 gms / 2¹/₃ cups*
Fennel (*saunf*) .... *10 gms / 2 tsp*
Clarified butter (*ghee*) .... *180 ml / ¾ cup*
Clarified butter to shallow fry
Milk .... *240 ml / 1¼ cup*
Salt to taste
Water .... *120 ml / ²/₃ cup*

METHOD:

1. Pound fennel with a pestle.
2. Sieve flour and salt together. Make a well in the flour and pour in milk and water. Mix gradually and knead into a dough. Cover with moist cloth and keep aside for 10 min.
3. Melt ¹/₃ of the clarified butter, add to the dough, kneading constantly to make it soft and smooth.
4. Add pounded fennel and knead again for 5 minutes.
5. Divide into 12 equal balls, dust lightly, roll into 6" discs. Apply 5 gms/1 tsp clarified butter evenly over one side.
6. Make a radial cut and fold disc into a narrow conical shape. Place flat side of the cone on palm and twist palms together in a round movement to compress dough into a thick flat round (*pedha*). Dust with flour, roll it out into an 8 inch disc. Refrigerate for an hour on butter paper.
8. Heat griddle and shallow fry both sides over low heat till golden.

TO SERVE:

Serve hot, accompanied by Raita (page 83) or any curry dish.

Picture on page 74

POORI

Unleavened puffed pancake—a north Indian speciality.

Serves: 4-5   **Prep. time:** 20 min   **Cooking time:** 10 min

INGREDIENTS:

Whole wheat flour .... *250 gms / 1¼ cups*
Oil .... *10 ml / 2 tsp*
Oil for deep frying
Salt to taste
Water .... *125 ml / ²/₃ cup*

METHOD:

1. Sieve the wheat flour and salt into a bowl. Add 10 ml of oil.
2. Make a well in the sieved flour, add cold water to it and gradually start mixing to form a fine hard dough.
3. Divide the dough into 25 equal size balls and place them on a lightly floured surface. Cover with a kitchen cloth for 5-10 minutes.
4. Flatten each ball between the palms to make a round, 4.5 cm in diameter. Roll out each of them to form an 6 cm disc.
5. Heat the oil and deep fry the pooris until they puff up.
6. Drain on a paper towel before serving.

TO SERVE:

Serve hot, as an accompaniment to any Indian curry.

TANDOORI ROTI

Oven-roasted bread.

Serves: 4-5 **Prep. time:** 40 min **Cooking time:** 5-8 min

INGREDIENTS:

Whole wheat flour .... *500 gms / 2½ cups*
Butter to grease baking tray
Oil .... *15 ml / 1 tbs*
Salt to taste
Water .... *300 ml / 1½ cups*

METHOD:

1. Sieve flour and salt in a mixing bowl. Add the water gradually, then the oil and knead to make a soft dough. Cover with a moist cloth, keep aside for half an hour.
2. Divide into 10 equal balls, dust with flour and keep aside covered.
3. Flatten each ball between the palms to about 15 cm in diameter. Bake for 3 minutes in a greased baking tray, in a pre-heated oven at 175 °C (350 °F) till pale brown in colour.

TO SERVE:

Serve hot, as an accompaniment to any curry dish.

Picture on page 74

KHASTA ROTI

Whole wheat oven-baked bread.

Serves: 4-5 **Prep. time:** 25 min **Cooking time:** 10-15 min

INGREDIENTS:

Whole wheat flour .... *500 gms / 2½ cups*
Carom seeds (*ajwain*) .... *15 gms / 1 tbs*
Salt to taste
Sugar .... *12 gms / 2½ tsp*
Water .... *300 ml / 1½ cups*

METHOD:

1. To the sieved flour, add salt, sugar and carom seeds. Knead into a hard dough with water. Cover with a moist cloth and keep aside for 15 minutes.
2. Divide the dough into 10 equal portions and roll into balls. Dust and roll into 10 cm rotis. Prick with a fork evenly.
3. Bake the rotis for 8-10 minutes in an oven at 175 °C (350 °F) or till light brown in colour.

TO SERVE:

Serve hot, as an accompaniment to any vegetable purée.

KHEER

This ever popular pudding has rice cooked on a slow fire in sweetened milk to make a rich, creamy dish.

Serves: 4   **Prep. time:** 1 hr   **Cooking time:** 1½ hrs

INGREDIENTS:

Milk	*1 litre / 4¼ cups*
Rice, long grain	*60 gms / ¼ cup*
Almonds	*15 gms / 1 tbs*
Cardamom powder	*5 gms / 1 tsp*
Clarified butter (*ghee*)	*10 ml / 2 tsp*
Milk to dissolve saffron	*30 ml / 2 tbs*
Raisins	*10 gms / 2 tsp*
Saffron	*a few strands*
Sugar	*120 gms / ²/₃ cup*

METHOD:

1. Wash and soak rice for an hour.
2. Blanch almonds. Cut into slivers.
3. Dissolve the saffron in warm milk and keep aside.
4. Boil milk in a *handi* (pot).
5. In another *handi* (pot) heat the clarified butter, add rice and stir fry for 4-5 minutes till it begins to brown lightly.
6. Add the milk and bring to boil, stirring constantly to prevent rice from sticking. Simmer till rice is cooked.
7. Stir in the sugar. Simmer till milk thickens.
8. Stir in cardamom powder, raisins and almonds.

TO SERVE:

Sprinkle saffron and serve hot in winter and cold in summer.

Facing page: Kheer

GAJRELA

Grated carrots cooked in thickened milk garnished with nuts and raisins.

Serves: 4   **Prep. time:** 30 min   **Cooking time:** 1 hr

INGREDIENTS:

Carrots, grated	*1 kg*
Milk	*1 litre / 4¼ cups*
Almonds, blanched and split	*20 gms / 4 tsp*
Clarified butter (*ghee*)	*100 ml / 7 tbs*
Fresh cream	*60 gms / 5 tbs*
Raisins	*15 gms / 1 tbs*
Sugar	*240 gms / 1¼ cups*

METHOD:

1. Boil milk in a *kadhai* (wok). Add the grated carrots and cook on medium heat, stirring constantly until the milk has thickened.
2. Stir in sugar and cook till most of the moisture has evaporated.
3. Add the clarified butter and cook for 5 minutes. Mix in the cream. Cook further for another 5 minutes. Remove from fire.

TO SERVE:

Serve hot, garnished with almonds and raisins.

Mango Kulfi

A mango and milk dessert. Always a welcome treat in the summer months.

Serves: 4-6   **Prep. time:** 20 min   **Cooking time:** 30 min
+ 8 hrs for setting

Ingredients:

Milk	*1 litre / 4¼ cups*
Mango pulp	*450 ml / 2¼ cups*
Double cream (heavy)	*150 ml / ¾ cup*
Sugar	*40 gms / 2²/₃ tbs*
Saffron	*a few strands*

Method:

1. Put milk into a heavy bottomed pan and bring to a boil. Lower heat and let it simmer.
2. Add sugar and cook the milk till quantity is reduced to a third and it is thick and creamy.
3. Add mango pulp and saffron, cook further for 2 minutes.
4. Cool to room temperature and mix in the cream.
5. Spoon the mixture into 6-8 moulds. Cover tightly with foil and freeze for at least 6 hours. Shake the mould thrice during first hour of freezing.

To Serve:

Remove from refrigerator, dip the bottom of the mould in hot water and invert onto a dish. Serve immediately.

Facing page: Mango Kulfi

Suji Halwa

Semolina dessert.

Serves: 4-6   **Prep. time:** 15 min   **Cooking time:** 15-20 min

Ingredients:

Semolina (*suji*)	*225 gms / 1 cup*
Almonds, blanched	*125 gms / ½ cup*
Butter (unsalted)	*225 gms / 1 cup*
Green Cardamom seeds, crushed	*4*
Sugar	*400 gms / 2 cups*
Sultanas or seedless raisins	*125 gms / ½ cup*
Water	*900 ml / 4½ cups*

Method:

1. Dissolve sugar in boiling water. Add crushed cardamom seeds and boil for 10 to 15 minutes till the mixture turns syrupy. Keep aside.
2. Melt butter in a second saucepan and stir in the semolina. On a medium flame, simmer mixture for 20 minutes, stirring continuously till semolina is light brown and crispy.
3. Add sultanas or seedless raisins, almonds and the sugar syrup stirring continuously and bring to boil. Cook and stir for another 5 minutes.

To Serve:

Pour mixture into a shallow dish and serve hot, or at room temperature.

Mint Relish

A fresh, green, tangy relish that is
Pudina Chutney *for you.*

Serves: 4   **Prep. time:** 20 min

Ingredients:

Mint leaves .... *60 gms / ¼ cup*
Coriander leaves .... *120 gms / ½ cup*
Cumin (*jeera*) .... *5 gms / 1 tsp*
Garlic cloves.. *2*
Green chilli.. *1*
Lemon juice (optional)* .... *5 gms / 1 tsp*
Raw mango, chopped .... *30 gms / 2 tbs*
Salt to taste
Tomatoes, chopped .... *45 gms / 3 tbs*

Method:

1. Clean, wash and chop coriander and mint. Slit and deseed green chillies.
2. Blend all ingredients in a food processor.
3. Pour into a dry jar and store in the refrigerator.

* Lemon juice may be added to make the relish tart.

To Serve:

A commonly used accompaniment to almost all Indian dishes.

Facing page: Mixed Raita

Mixed Raita

A delicious yoghurt preparation.

Serves: 4   **Prep. time:** 30 min   **Cooking time:** 5 min

Ingredients:

Yoghurt .... *600 gms / 3 cups*
Black peppercorns .... *2½ gms / ½ tsp*
Chilli powder to sprinkle .... *a pinch*
Coriander seeds... *5 gms / 1 tsp*
Cucumber, chopped .... *30 gms / 2 tbs*
Cumin (*jeera*) seeds.................................. *5 gms / 1 tsp*
Green chilli, finely chopped .... *5 gms / 1 tsp*
Mint, chopped .... *5 gms / 1 tsp*
Onions, chopped .... *30 gms / 2 tbs*
Salt to taste
Tomatoes, chopped .... *30 gms / 2 tbs*

Method:

1. Heat a *tawa* (griddle), roast cumin, coriander seeds and pepper till dark and aromatic. Pound and keep aside.
2. Whisk yoghurt with salt. Stir in all chopped items.
3. Pour into a bowl. Sprinkle with chilli powder and the pounded spices. Chill before serving.

To Serve:

A favourite accompaniment to all dishes, curry or kebab.
Note: Add pineapple chunks (60 gms/4 tbs) for variation.

INDEX